contents

instant attraction

introductions

How often is it that we come across a new material? Lots of products come along, but rarely do we find something that is really versatile and fun to work with – from mega-glitzy moments to more grown up reflections.

My 'affair' with Angelina began during my first visit to Art Van Go's studio and shop in Knebworth. Viv Arthur suggested that I have a little play with a new fibre she had recently added to her stock. Packages of glowing iridescent colours, from deep blue, greens and corals to lime greens, the brightest acid yellow and wild pinks.

Angelina fibres have a little bit of magic in them – especially for those of us who have laboured over felting! All you had to do (I was assured) was to lay out the fibres between thin paper and iron! Lo and behold – out from between the sheets appeared a fully formed fabric – lustrous and iridescent. Leaving with a packet or two clutched tightly I promised to have a try and see where it led me.

Back at my studio a fun time ensued.

I was teaching a course soon afterwards, which involved making a series of surfaces with bonded sheers, fibres and plastics and the Angelina fitted very neatly into this. After this point I had to discover a bit more about these fibres – what else could they do?

Well, as it turns out they can do quite a lot! Blending colours, over-heating, melting, painting, gilding, stitching, adding into felt and silk fibres, spinning, etc., etc.

The purpose in writing this book will have been fulfilled if what you find here helps you to enjoy using a novel material. **Instant Attraction**, **Angelina Laid Bare**, **Playing the Field** and **Caught - Hook, Line & Stitch** will lead you through specific skills to use the Angelina fibres. In these sections the information is organised according to the techniques being discussed. Of course, having read this and tried a few ideas, you should feel free to experiment with the fibres and discover your own favourite effects and the uses which are most relevant to your own style of working.

Testing the Water gives details of projects. which I hope will encourage you to make particular pieces using a range of the properties of the Angelina. You can follow these projects exactly like a recipe, but with so many variations, you might equally want to alter the colours and designs to suit your personal style. Whether you follow directions exactly or use these for guidance adding flourishes and styles of your own, you should find something new.

Indeed, no matter how may times I teach a class, someone finds a novel and exciting combination which I had not happened upon before, so … happy experimenting.

Finally, **Hot Dates** is a small gallery, showing work by selected artists (including me, inevitably!) who have utilised the Angelina fibres in a variety of ways. Angelina is often incorporated into other materials, making use of the great diversity of possibilities, yet retaining the basic properties of the fibres. Perhaps this section will spur your thoughts on to more individual projects. Think how you might make Angelina a part of your work.

Having spent over a year 'between the sheets with Angelina', it is a pleasure to introduce you to her. I hope that during the reading of this book, you will discover a few new tricks and games to enjoy – either on your own or in the company of others – she is there to share!

Alysn Midgelow-Marsden

2

getting aquainted

According to the manufacturer, Angelina Fibre 'is an exciting new development in the world of textile fibres that will revolutionise the use of sparkle in all fabrics'. That aside for a moment, it is true that the fibres and their properties are so different from anything else you can use to add 'sparkle', that for some, the revolutionary appeal will be true and there are so many possibilities that there has to be some application for everyone!

The fibre has a supersoft handle, much like cashmere, but has been produced in such a way that even just a little added to another fibre mix will result in a sparkling effect.

Angelina Fibre can be spun, woven, layered, trapped, bonded, etc. Its applications in textile art, embroidery, papermaking, papier mache, modelling, card and candle making, etc. are endless!

Art Van Go is delighted to make available in the UK probably the most innovative selection from the Angelina range.

The iridescent polyester fibres of 'Hot Fix' Angelina will bond to themselves at relatively low temperatures to produce a non-woven type of fabric. Bonding occurs when the 'Hot Fix' fibres soften and fuse together. The 15 denier fibres that Art Van Go supply are the finest available and make the softest sheets of fabric possible.

The colour range includes:

Blaze, Cobalt Sparkle, Forest Blaze, Wisteria, Pink Tickle, Raspberry, Peacock, Ultra Violet, Sugar Plum, Key Lime, Lemon Sparkle, Mint Sparkle and Calypso Blue.

There is also a range of 'Standard' and 'Metallic' fibres available, which will not fuse at the low temperatures that can be achieved in our workrooms, but which have interesting uses and combinations nonetheless. These will be important to us later in the book. Colours available in this type of fibre include: Gold, Silver, Gunmetal and Bronze polyester fibres; Metallic Copper and Metallic Turquoise aluminium fibres.

An added advantage of Angelina is that because the fibres are polyester or aluminium, they are washable (though I only hand wash them) and dry very quickly.

One word of caution – do not re-iron after making the fibre, for reasons which will be obvious once you have read the book! In fact the fabric tends to dry flat anyway so this is not a problem.

Given that we are all such individual workers and each have our favoured techniques and finished items, the list of possible ideas for items to make using Angelina could go on for ever, so here is a small section of ideas that might spur your imagination:

Bags	Jewellery
Ballerina Costumes	Knitting
Book covers	Lampshades
Box tops	Mirror Frames
Corsages	Paper Making
Couture	Picture frames
Christmas Ornaments	Spinning
Collages	Shawls
Crochet	Sculpture
Embellishments	Trimmings
Felting	Theatre Projects
Floral arrangements	Veils
Greetings cards	Wedding Dresses and favours
Gift packaging	Weaving
Hair ornaments	

And no doubt more.
The key is to explore!

3

All you need to get started

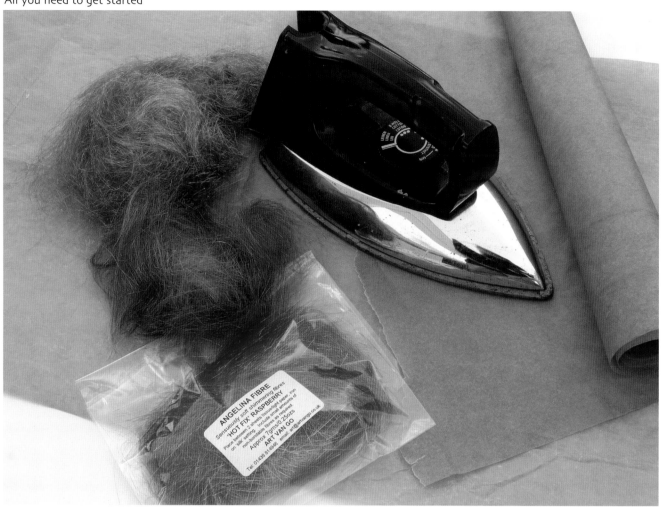

Safe steps

The Angelina fibres are completely non-toxic when used in the ways described in most sections. If in any section there are particular safety considerations, they will be highlighted in '**safe steps**' boxes just like this one.

Do be careful not to catch yourself on the hot plate of the iron whilst using it. (We've all done that in moments of excitement!)

warming to the occasion

The best way to start is by testing the procedure on a small amount of fibre. You will very soon get the feel of the process and then have the confidence to try the other techniques.

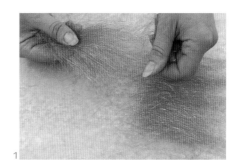

1 Place a sheet of baking parchment onto an ironing surface (ironing board or a cloth on a table), then take a small amount of the fibres and lay out onto the parchment to the size of fabric you wish to make.

2 Lay another piece of baking parchment over the fibres and using an iron set to the 'silk' setting, gently move the iron back and forth over the surface of the paper. Press down firmly, but don't spend more than 2 or 3 seconds in contact to start with.

3 The fibres should bond quickly, so check frequently to see the progress. Too much heat or pressure can change the original qualities of the fibre (as you will see later).

Generally, at low temperatures 'Hot Fix' Angelina will only bond to itself not to other fibres or paper. The result will be a sheet of web-like non-woven sparkling fabric that is peeled off the paper.

If the fibres have not fused into a sheet, it requires a slightly longer time ironing.

   If the fibres continue not to bond it may be necessary to increase the temperature on the iron slightly as the temperatures of the settings do vary a little.

   Avoid using too hot a setting to start with as this will affect the overall result.

An eye-catching selection of 'Hot Fix' fibres and fused sheets

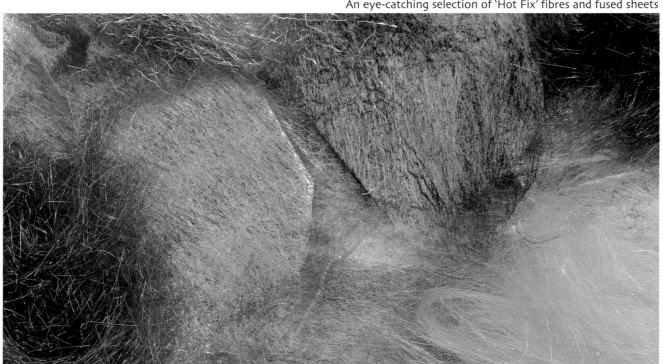

Angelina laid bare

Having made a sheet or two of the basic fabric, we are now ready to think about playing with this. You will already have asked yourself: How much fibre is the right amount? Do the fibres need to be laid out neatly? Do I have to stick with one colour of fibre at a time?

For the answers – read on!

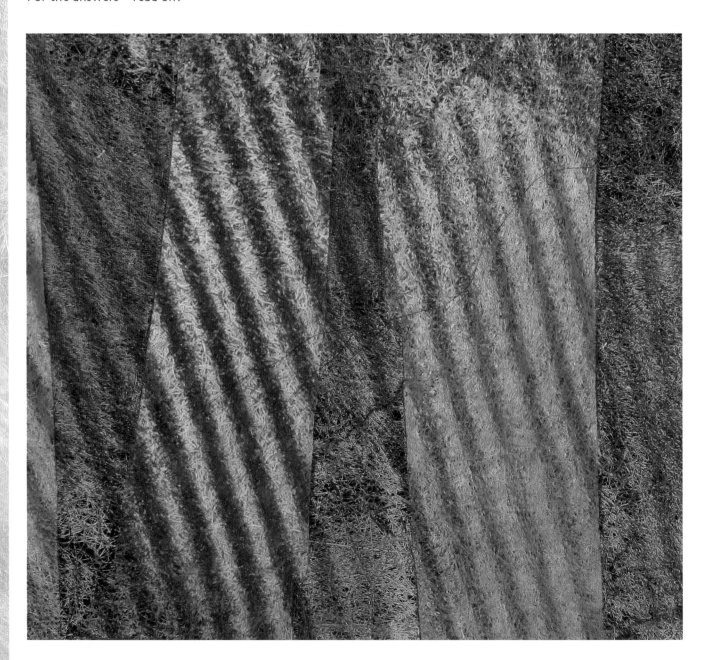

a bit of a tease?

There is no 'right' amount of fibres to make your Angelina fabric. So long as there are overlaps between the fibres you can produce an incredibly fine and delicate web-like fabric, which would be lovely overlaid onto a contrasting background or suspended in a frame or card aperture. When using the Angelina very finely, take great care with the dwell time of your iron on the fibres as they take very little heating to fuse.

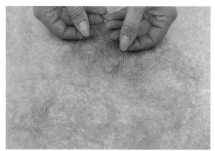

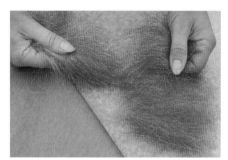

Fine and delicate

Or you can pile up the fibres quite densely and produce a solid fabric more like a sheet of card, which can be cut and applied over other work or painted on, etc.

When using the Angelina fibres very thickly it will probably be necessary to iron the sheet on both sides to fully fuse the fibres.

Thick and dense

The absolute limit will come when the amount of heat needed to penetrate into the fibre pile is so great that the outer fibres lose their iridescence and become matt.

Shaken or stirred?

As with so many situations, the answer to this question depends on the effect you want to achieve.

If you would like a neat fabric with an even density, then spread the fibres evenly by pulling them from the mass in a straight pull as for laying fibres when felting or making silk papers.

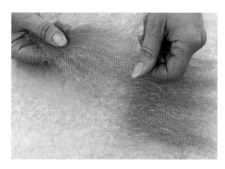

If you want a more swirly, haphazard look and a fabric that has both dense and lightweight areas, then allow the fibres to fall, or play with the patterns they make on the baking parchment before ironing.

Mixing in

Why stop at one colour? The fibres can be blended for shimmering multi-coloured effects and with such a range of combinations available, who could resist giving it a go?

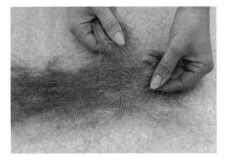

You could completely mix two or more colours together by pulling your chosen selection apart again and again, like shuffling a deck of cards, to blend the colours before laying out and ironing them.

Create shimmering rainbows and colour transformations by grading the fibres from one colour to another, to another, to another .....

it's all in the length

The fibre length from the packet is approximately 4" (10cm), but there is absolutely no reason to leave them at that length, get your scissors out and give them the chop!

The resulting fabric will have a different look and the possibilities for colour mixing and introducing patterns into the fabric will be tremendously increased.

The fibres can be as short as you wish so long as there is still some overlap between the strands.

affairs of the heat

Useful equipment

In this section you will be dealing with not only hot irons, but also naked flames from both candles and gas flames as well as red hot metal wires.

You should take all precautions to protect yourself from possible burns and always work with a bowl of water nearby in case the volatile Angelina sheet catches fire – BE WARNED this probably **will** happen at some stage in these experiments.

Also, as with any man made material, when the fibres melt they give off fumes which not only smell bad but should not be inhaled. Ideally these experiments should be carried out in a fume cupboard. If this is not possible, work in a well-ventilated room with a respirator and for short periods of time. If at any time you feel uncomfortable, stop and leave the area until the fumes have dispersed.

You will have noticed by now, whether by accident or by design, that the amount of heat applied to the fibres can have an effect in addition to that of fusing the fibres together. Depending upon the amount of heat added, the fibres also react by changing colours. The effects can be more or less pronounced depending upon the fibre, the amount of heat and the way in which the heat is applied. Also, being a man made fibre, we are able to melt and burn the sheet (in a controlled fashion we hope) to produce other interesting and useful effects.

hot all over

Try leaving your iron on some Angelina (under the baking parchment of course) for a longer time than you have become used to doing, also try turning the heat of the iron up slightly, to the 'wool' setting to start with, then hotter if you feel the need, and see the difference it makes to the 'Hot Fix' colours.

Some of the fibres show a more pronounced colour change than others. For instance the peacock, wisteria and ultra violet can all change to give a more greenish-gold or purple-like hue; raspberry and pink tickle can become more coral coloured; limes can become more gold, etc. Both the temperature and a longer time in contact with the heat will affect the colour, and eventually the colours will lose their brilliance and become dull. This property will become really useful later.

Interesting effects can be achieved by folding the original sheet into pleats and then re-ironing. This will reduce the iridescence of the fibres, but the sheet will, to some extent, fuse together again, though not as completely as the original fusing.

Heat effects on Pink Tickle

Pleated and re-ironed

bubbling with excitement

If you CAREFULLY (and I do mean CAREFULLY in large, friendly letters), lower a sheet of fused Angelina towards a candle flame, holding it by a pair of tweezers or even better between two pairs of tweezers, you will find that the fabric softens and begins to distort whilst you are still up to 5" (13cm) away from the flame.

Then move your fabric away from the heat and allow it to cool before touching. The Angelina, being a man made fibre, will melt and deform in a way similar to plastic or nylon fabric, etc.

Don't forget to work with a container of water nearby at all times whilst bubbling the fabric in case it catches light.

Bubbling can either be gently controlled allowing you to retain some of the iridescence of the original fibres, or you can be more forceful and allow the fabric to become more molten and web-like.

A craft heat gun may also be used to achieve bubbling and texturing. Make sure that you use a non-flammable surface under the Angelina you are heating and melting.

Melting Moments

Taking a pre-made sheet of Angelina, you can melt the edges by carefully offering the edge of the sheet to a candle flame.

Hold with tweezers and remember to have water nearby. Because the Angelina is very heat sensitive, the edge will melt when you are still quite a distance from the flame possibly as far as 5" (13cm).

Angelina tends to catch fire if you get too close, therefore it is particularly important to be ready to take the piece away from the candle and blow out the section which has caught fire or dip the Angelina into the water.

Remember, the molten edges are extremely hot – do not touch these edges for a few seconds until they have re-solidified and cooled.

hot wired

You may already have a favourite method of burning through man-made fibres, and there are plenty of methods possible. These might include jos sticks, soldering irons, hot wires, pyrography tools and no doubt more.

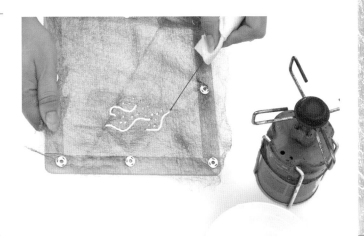

My personal preference is to heat a medium weight florists' wire (not one wrapped in plastic) in a strong gas flame. I use a camping gas flame which is eminently portable and can be placed near to a sink with water very easily, but you can also use the flame on a gas hob or similar. Though it is probably best not to do this whilst you are preparing food!

Place your prepared sheet of Angelina into a frame to hold the sheet steady. Making sure that the section of wire you will be holding is well wrapped in something like kitchen towel to protect your hand from the heat travelling through the wire, heat until the tip of the wire is red hot and then use this as a pen to melt patterns and shapes into the fabric.

As the wire cools you will feel that it begins to drag. Simply place the wire back into the flame to reheat, then continue.

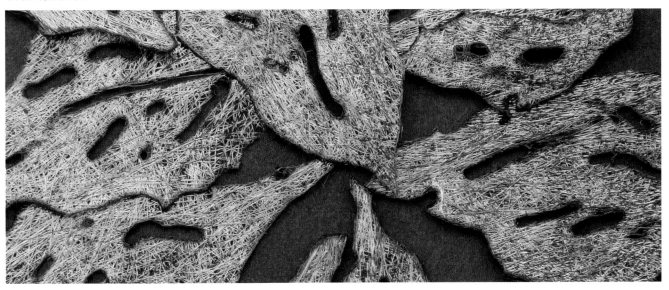

making a good impression

Here, we use a stunningly simple and effective way to make a great use of the colour changing properties of the 'Hot Fix' Angelina fibres.

Any surface with a hard firm texture or pattern that can be placed under the Angelina during the ironing process will make a permanent impression on the finished Angelina sheet.

The raised areas of the textured surface will have kept the Angelina in close contact with the heat of the iron, causing these fibres to be more affected by the heat.

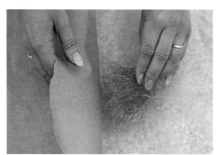

Place your object or textured surface (examples would be metal meshes, thick lace or wooden print blocks) onto the baking parchment then 'Hot Fix' Angelina fibres onto the top. You will need sufficient to make a fairly solid fabric rather than a very delicate sprinkle of fibres.

Place the other sheet of baking parchment over the top and iron firmly.

Here's a tip....
When using the small print blocks you will find there are quite a lot of the Angelina fibres left around the edges. These can be left as a part of the work, or trimmed away and used to make other pieces of fabric or impressions – no need to waste them.

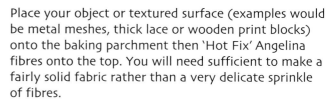

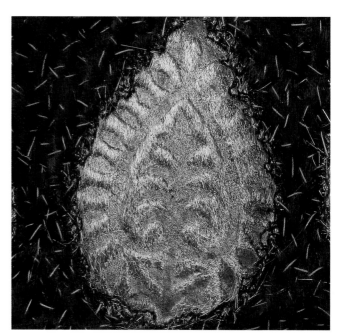

in a twist

For those amongst you (yes, I know you are out there) who are just a little twisted, the fibres lend themselves very nicely to being spun and plied into a yarn - either 'Hot Fix' alone, 'Standard' alone or a mixture (read on to discover about these other family members).

Plying could be with the same colour or another one to make interesting mixtures of threads.

The metallic fibres are more of a challenge as they don't have the same easy handleability as the polyester fibres.

Once spun and plied, they can be used as any yarn, whatever takes your fancy! Knitting, crocheting, macramé, couching, etc. The threads are a little 'twisty' on themselves but not unbearably so.

Keeping it in the family

Up until this point, apart from vague hints, we have not yet introduced you to 'Hot Fix' Angelina's sisters! They have been patiently waiting in the wings whilst you to get to know their more showy and out-going sister.

So now is the time to meet 'Standard' and 'Metallic' fibres. Due to their make-up, the 'Hot Fix' colours are not produced in metallic shades. The non-bondable, 'Standard' and 'Metallic' colours, are included as a separate section to complement the 'Hot Fix' range.

The 'Standard' fibres are 8 denier and have a 4" (10cm) length with the same super-soft handle. They can be spun, woven, included in papermaking, etc. just like the 'Hot Fix' fibres, but they will not bond to themselves at low temperatures.

At a much higher temperature the 'Standard' fibres will melt into each other, but will lose their softness. The 'Metallic' fibres are made from fine aluminium and feel different (rather like pan scrubbers actually!), and also will not bond to themselves.
The colours available include:Gold, Bronze, Silver, Gunmetal , Metallic Copper & Metallic Turquoise

'Standard' or 'Metallic' Fibres can be combined with 'Hot Fix' to give an added metallic 'glitz'. The trick is to lay a quantity of 'Hot Fix' fibres down onto baking parchment, add a smaller quantity of the 'Standard' or 'Metallic' fibre over these, making sure the fibres are spread and open (not in clumps) and add another layer of 'Hot Fix' over the top. Heat to bond the fibres in the normal way. The non-'Hot Fix' fibres are then trapped within the fabric and will remain stable unless so much is used that it cannot be successfully held by the 'Hot Fix'. In this case, the non-'Hot Fix' fibres will loosen out of the fabric if rubbed and pulled. With this in mind, a more stable fabric may be achieved if the fibres are mixed together by hand.

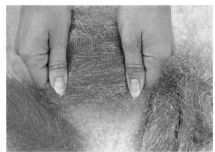
Hand mixing fibres

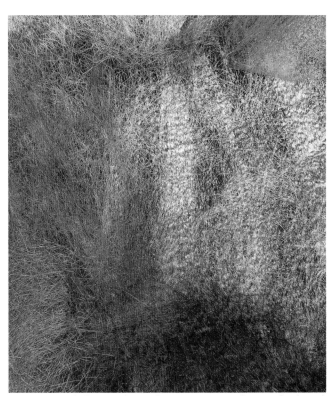
Mixed sheets of Angelina 'Hot Fix' with 'Standard' and 'Metallic' fibres

The proportions you use to make a sheet of the mixed 'Hot Fix' and 'Standard' or 'Metallic' can be allowed to vary tremendously, and the effect achieved by doing so will also be different. By using a small amount of 'Standard' or 'Metallic' fibres mixed between a larger amount of 'Hot Fix' fibres, you are able to modify the look of the colour of the 'Hot Fix' fibres. A possible ratio of 1 part 'Standard'/'Metallic' fibres to 5 parts 'Hot Fix' fibres will achieve this sort of subtle modification of the 'Hot Fix' colour. Adding larger proportions of the 'Standard'/'Metallic' fibres will achieve a more pronounced effect accordingly, through to the opposite extreme where you might be using something in the region of a 5 parts 'Standard'/'Metallic' to 1 part of 'Hot Fix' fibre. The resulting fabric is held fairly lightly by the 'Hot Fix' fibres fusing together in a mesh around the 'Standard'/'Metallic' and this then results in a fabric which is almost the colour of the 'Standard'/'Metallic' fibres alone.

We can go one stage further in accentuating the colour of the 'Standard'/'Metallic' – we can overheat the fabric as we make it, so that the iridescence in the 'Hot Fix' fibres is lost.

In this case it may be almost impossible (if you didn't know they were there) to see the 'Hot Fix' fibres at all.

'Hot Fix' Forest Blaze with 'Standard' Bronze, upper section has been ironed to fix, the lower section has been re-ironed

playing the field

painted lady

If you want to change the colour of the Angelina fibres in ways other than mixing coloured fibres or heating, then you will need to consider methods of getting the colour to stick to the fibres.

As Angelina is a polyester, we are left with considering colouring techniques that are either designed specifically for man-made fibres, such as transfer paints, or those which will coat the outside of the fibre, such as acrylics. Once you have coloured the fabrics you can use them in any way you wish: cutting, applying, melting, stitching, etc. You will have created an original surface and look of fabric that you can exploit in your own way.

Useful materials

Try simply rolling, painting or stencilling onto the Angelina fabric with acrylic paints or other paints in a binding medium such as PVA or acrylic varnish etc., leaving some of the iridescence and shimmer of the original colour to peek through.

Also have fun by mixing texture gels with sand, fibres, mica or other granules held in a binding medium, into your paints. This will add interesting heights and forms to the fabric.

Think about adding bronze powders or iridescent pigments into the binders to achieve additional effects. I particularly like to use texture gels and contrasting colours on a roller over the fabric.

Acrylics

Relief outliners such as those used for appliqué, silk or in glass painting can be used to draw onto the sheet of Angelina in fairly fine detail.

Relief outliner

Solid bar paints such as oil pastels, heat-fixable Lithocoal® and ChromaCoal™, oil bars such as Markal® and gilding waxes such as Treasure Gold® and Jewels®, can all be rubbed onto the surface of the Angelina either freely or through stencils. The most effective of these seem to be those that will rub on with the least abrasion, so that the surface of the fabric is not damaged in the process.

Markal® paint sticks

Because transfer paints (also known as disperse dyes) are designed to work on man-made fibres they will affect the colour of the Angelina fibres, the downside being that the heat required to transfer the dye from the paper to the fabric can be hotter than the 'Hot Fix' Angelina can stand whilst retaining it's shimmering quality.

Transfer dyes are first painted onto a sheet of paper, checking with the instructions for any dilutions necessary. When dry, either the whole sheet, ripped or cut sections of the paper are then placed face down onto the Angelina fabric, baking parchment over the top and then ironed. The colour on the paper will transfer onto the fabric. This method of colouring will not show effectively on the darker colours.

Fabric transfer crayons also work in the same way.

Transfer dyes

Useful materials

There are many ways to gild surfaces and many effects to learn. However, for the purpose of this book, we will stick to those that achieve quick effects with ease and do not require specialist mediums or expensive precious metals.

So, we will look at metal leaf (an imitation 'gold' leaf available in a range of golds, silver and copper) sold as 'Dutch Metal' or 'Schlag'. The version that comes on a light paper carrier sheet is the easiest to handle in this situation. It is a very fine sheet of metal, which can be gilded on to non-absorbent surfaces with 'size'.

We will also use transfer foils, which are not metal leaf but a metallic plastic attached to a clear plastic carrier sheet and which will also adhere to 'size'. They will also adhere onto some other surfaces when simply ironed over.

Transfer foils are available in various forms and a wide range of colours from the traditional metal colour through bright metallic colours such as reds, greens and purples, to multicoloured sheets in different patterns and ending in wild holographic patterns.

Both metal leaf and transfer foils have their place in the greater scheme of embellishing surfaces and both give a different type of effect, so, once again, it's down to you to try them out and decide which effect to use for which occasion.

1

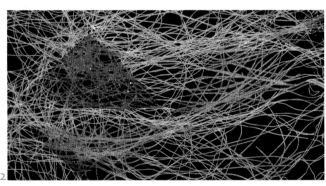

2

hot under the sheet

Using the transfer foils is the most instant form of gilding.

1/2 Placing transfer foil onto Angelina fabric and ironing directly will, with some transfer foils, allow the foil to adhere directly to the Angelina fibres, though this may seem to diminish the effect of the Angelina fibres themselves.

You may prefer to paint PVA onto the areas you wish to gild, allow to dry, then place the transfer foil, coloured face up, onto the Angelina, lay baking parchment over that and iron as quickly as possible over the surface.

Some transfer foils like the iron to be a little hotter than is ideal for the 'Hot Fix' Angelina, so take care and be fairly gentle with the iron so that it touches the PVA'd areas rather than the fibres as much as you can.

Leave this to cool for a few seconds before pulling the transfer foil away from the Angelina sheet.

It is also possible to use a layer of transfer adhesive to adhere metal leaf to the Angelina fabric, but take care that the ironing temperature needed to activate the transfer adhesive may be higher than ideal for the 'Hot Fix' Angelina fibres.

3 Relief outliners can be drawn onto your Angelina sheet in all sorts of patterns and allowed to dry for up to a day.

Once dry, repeat the process described above and the transfer foil will adhere to the relief outliner.

4

4 Lithocoal® and Chromacoal™ are charcoal and pastel substitutes for artists who do not want to use spray fixatives on their work. They are heat-fixed with an iron. We can use this property to enable transfer foil to stick to the Lithocoal®/ChromaCoal™ and the Lithocoal®/ChromaCoal™ to stick to the Angelina fabric all in one easy step, at the same time creating interesting effects. Great fun!

Lay your Angelina fabric onto the baking parchment and either make thick crayon marks with the Lithocoal®/ChromaCoal™ or crumble the end onto the fabric (it is a naturally soft and crumbly medium). Place a sheet of transfer foil over this (remember – colour side up), then more baking parchment, then iron.

Allow that few seconds for the sandwich to cool down and pull the transfer foil away from the surface. You should have little sparkling nuggets where the Lithocoal®/ChromaCoal™ was.

Here's a tip.....
If the crumbles are too large they will drop off the fabric. A quick trial will show you how big is too big, and how thick is thick.

sizing up Angelina

When we use metal leaf, we use 'size' instead of PVA. This is a type of glue and the one we shall use has an acrylic base rather than the traditional animal-based glues. The unique character of this glue is that, unlike PVA, which it resembles in other respects, it dries clear but retains its stickiness indefinitely, so that anything, especially fine metal leaf will adhere to it.

In brief, all that is needed to gild the Angelina fabric is for the surface to be sized and then the metal leaf can be simply rubbed on.

This method can also be used with some of the transfer foils.

Here's a tip …..
The metal leaf will be easier to handle if you rub a little talc onto your hands before starting.

If the Angelina fabric is quite fine and mesh-like, the surface areas that you wish to gild will first require painting with acrylic paint, varnish, PVA or similar to give the size something to hang onto. Otherwise, not enough size will stay attached to the fine fibres for the metal leaf or transfer foil to stick to.

Coat the areas you wish to gild with size and allow to dry.

Place the sheet of metal leaf or foil over the sized area and burnish it with your fingers.

The metal leaf carrier sheet can now be lifted away and the metallic surface will stay on your fabric.

The metal leaf left on the fabric will need a firm but soft brushing to both encourage the metal to stick to the sized areas and to brush away the surplus.

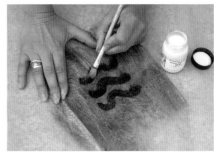

Coat the areas you wish to gild with size and allow to dry

Place the sheet of metal leaf or foil over the sized area and burnish it with your fingers

The metal leaf carrier sheet can now be lifted away and the metallic surface will stay on your fabric

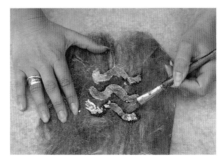

The metal leaf left on the fabric will need a firm but soft brushing to both encourage the metal to stick to the sized areas and to brush away the surplus

Useful materials

Though 'Hot Fix' Angelina will only bond to itself, the mesh this creates is able to very effectively trap other lightweight and relatively flat materials in a kind of sandwich. This allows us to make some really interesting surfaces.

Lay a fine(ish) layer of 'Hot Fix' Angelina onto your parchment. There is no precise 'right' amount, it really comes down to having sufficient fibres to trap the additions without obscuring them.

Then add a random sprinkling or a defined pattern of your sandwich fillings over this. Add another layer of 'Hot Fix' Angelina over the top. Place the baking parchment over this and iron as normal.

You may find it necessary to turn your sandwich over and give another quick iron on the other side to fully fuse the fibres under your fillings. Here are a few ideas of materials to try. No doubt you will be able to think of more.

Sandwiching materials into the Angelina

Fibres such as silk fibres, noils, throwsters waste, flax and linen

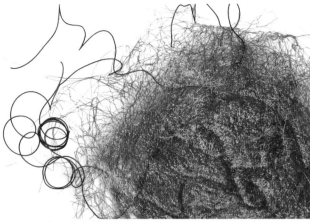

Wires such as beading wire or fine craft wires. If these are too heavy they will tend to pull out. It helps if the wires have bends or twists added so that they don't pull out as easily

Feathers, petals, dried flowers, grasses, skeleton leaves

Threads, hand or machine, smooth or textured

Irise paper table decorations or flakes

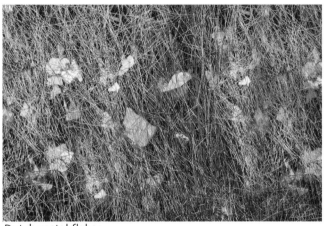

Dutch metal flakes

Snips of sheer fabrics or silk/metal tissue

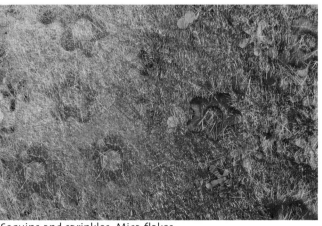

Sequins and sprinkles, Mica flakes

Useful materials

wrapped up in each other

Now let's look at trapping from another perspective.

Rather than sandwiching small pieces of fibres, etc. between layers of 'Hot Fix' Angelina, we need to think of using the Angelina the opposite way round. These ideas involve adding a small amount of Angelina during the processes of papermaking, felting and silk paper making in all its guises. This gives a little extra embedded sparkle.

Whilst we don't have space here to go through the processes of the various craft forms mentioned, there are suggested books in **Keeping in Touch** to give you those details and loads of other advice.

In a fine silk paper, half ironed and half not – see if you can spot the difference

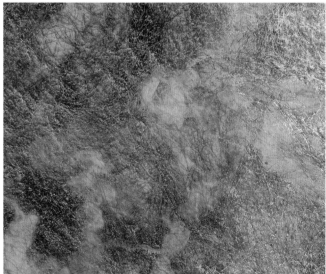

In a textured silk paper

In a thicker silk paper

Into cocoon strippings

making an attachment

Now that you have made and decorated sheets of Angelina – how might you make use of them?

As they will not voluntarily stick to anything other than themselves, we have to find ways of bonding them to other surfaces. The most straightforward method for collages and similar projects is to use PVA or fabric glues. But when we want to be able to attach our fibres onto fine surfaces such as sheer fabrics, we can use the heat bondable glues such as transfer adhesive (for example 'Bondaweb') or bonding powder. If used carefully, these will allow us to achieve a variety of effects onto other surfaces whether we are working on card, paper or fabric. These ideas are fine for the 'Standard' and 'Metallic' fibres as they do not react to the heat. Using the 'Hot Fix' fibres can be more tricky, as the iron generally needs to be set higher to melt these glues than required to affect the 'Hot Fix' fibres.

1 Start with simply laying down a layer of transfer adhesive with the backing removed, or sprinkle some bonding powder onto the surface you are wishing to adhere to, then a layer of Angelina fibres. Cover with parchment and iron.

You may find it more controllable on a thinner surface to reverse the layers so that the 'Hot Fix' Angelina is underneath and the surface to which you are sticking them is on the top. This way the Angelina is not directly in contact with the iron and more heat can be applied before the fibres lose their lustre. On a thick surface such as card, wood, metal or leather you just have to be very careful to apply the heat for as little time as possible – so a good firm hot iron for a brief time is best.

2a Alternatively, if you want to achieve lovely, lacy, delicate effects then we can work slightly differently. Place a sheet of transfer adhesive down, leaving the paper backing in place. Place a very small amount of Angelina onto the surface over any other bits and pieces that are lightweight in nature, such as threads, skeleton leaves or sprinkles. The whole effect needs to be kept light and lacy, both to achieve the best look and to allow the transfer adhesive to hold onto the fibres, etc.

2b Cover your piece with parchment and iron lightly to catch the layers together.

2c Then cut sections or shapes from this sheet. If necessary use the paper backing to draw out your designs, so cutting intricate designs is easy to follow.

2d/2e Remove the paper backing. Take these sections of decorated transfer adhesive and add to another background by ironing. The transfer adhesive requires a slightly higher heat than is ideal for the 'Hot Fix' fibres, so be careful. Any background will work – try paper, satins, sheer fabrics, etc. This technique makes a lovely surface for cards, collage or appliqué as it is, or as a surface to stitch into.

You may wish to 'play around' layering Angelina fibres, fabrics, threads, wires, etc. onto some of the laminating films available. These work rather like a one-sided transfer adhesive.

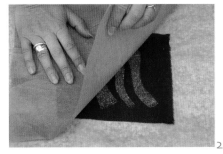

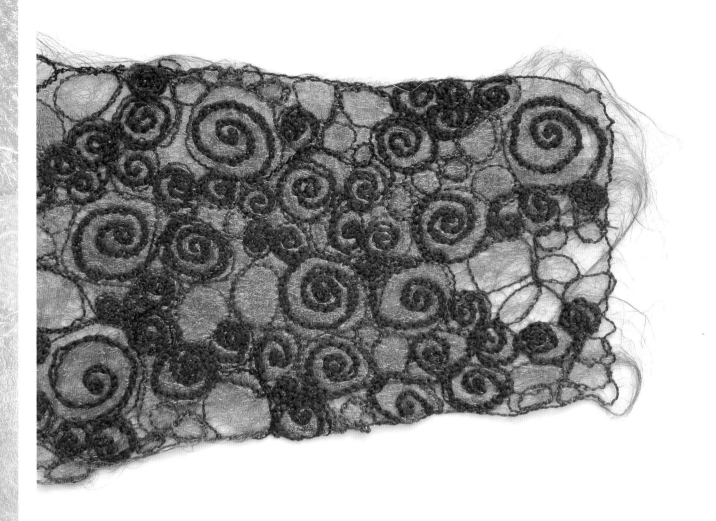

caught - hook, line & stitch

- Angelina all over
- Angelina on top
- stuck on you
- dissolving in anticipation

For the stitchers, this is the moment you have been waiting for. The intention has been to lead you through many ideas to create those scrummy, sassy surfaces, which can now be further embellished with stitch. Otherwise, you could stitch then embellish with any of the ideas previously covered.

So, I hope the getting here has been fun and that you feel confident and ready to stitch!

These next few pages will help you to really get to grips with incorporating Angelina fibres into embroidered textile pieces.

I can't emphasise enough, as with the other sections, these are just ideas, you should be prepared to try these and then move further forward in your own way.

Angelina all over

Try using the Angelina fabric as a whole piece and stitch into the surface, either by hand or machine or a mixture.

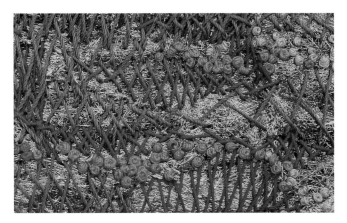

It is possible with some care to stitch directly through the Angelina fabric, though it is much easier to control if you use a backing of some kind. Stitch-N-Tear® or lightweight sew-in Vilene™ or other stabilising backings are fine if your sheet of Angelina is thick enough not to be seen through.

If your Angelina sheet is quite fine and any backing will be seen, then you can use a cold water soluble fabric laid behind your Angelina. When no longer required it can be washed away.

If you have made inclusions such as paper or other materials that would not be stable if immersed in water, the finest soluble fabrics work well and require only the lightest of sprays from a water spray to dissolve the sheet away.

Pin or tack the backing into place. If you wish to use a frame, I recommend using a flat embroidery frame and securing your work with silk pins as this won't stretch or stress the Angelina as a hoop could.

Then stitch! Whatever and however you like!

I particularly like the effect of adding sufficient stitching or embellishment so that the patterns of the stitching become the important factor and the sheen of the Angelina fabric is the background for that.

Angelina on top

Another little bit of magical fun!

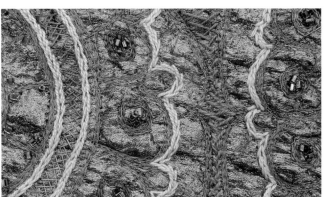

Once we start to think about laying the Angelina onto a background, the question of colour comes up. It is an intriguing question because the Angelina fabrics, especially those made mostly from 'Hot Fix' fibres, have chameleon-like tendencies.

Try laying a sheet of any Angelina colour onto different backgrounds and you will soon see what I mean. The whole tone of the piece will be completely altered by the background colour as you can see.

Angelina fabric is rarely completely opaque, so the colour showing through the fabric from the background will highlight a different aspect of the colours found in the fibres.

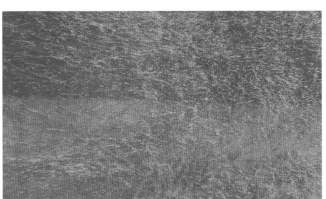

It is both rewarding and often necessary to spend time laying your Angelina fabric onto a variety of coloured backgrounds and being prepared to be surprised.

Having found a suitable partner for your Angelina, you can now cut sections of the Angelina sheet (or more than one colour, or with bits trapped, or painted or gilded, etc. etc.) and arrange on the background. It is usually fine to pin into place, but if the background fabric is slippery or stretchy it may be best to tack the pieces into place before you begin.

To secure the pieces you might use hand stitching or straight machine lines, satin stitch, automatic patterns or free machine embroidery. Then carry on with additional stitching, beading or other finishing processes as you wish.

Also remember that the sheet does not have to be applied flat onto the background but can be scrunched or padded to add texture.

stuck on you

If you are not into stitch, but want to achieve an appliquéd effect, lay your base fabric onto a non-stick paper such as baking parchment, cut sections of Angelina fabric, arrange them onto the background fabric, then squeeze a line of relief outliner around the shapes in order to attach them to the background.

You can then make more patterns or swirls, etc. to link the applied areas together and increase the effectiveness of the surface.

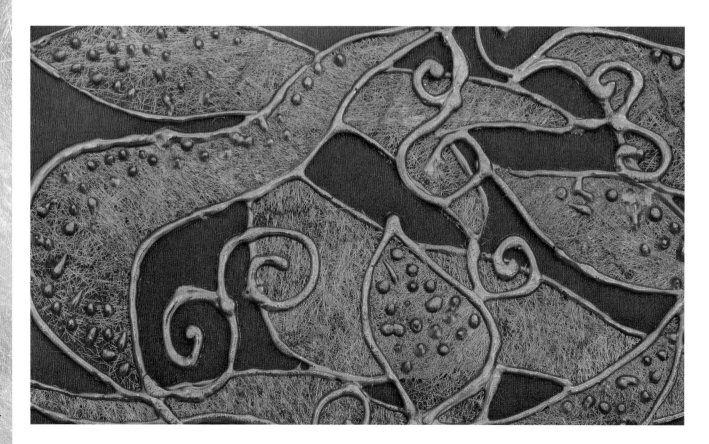

dissolving passions

These ideas all exploit the possibilities offered through the use of soluble fabric or films, of which there are many. I suggest limiting your options to the cold water dissolve varieties. Most of the ideas suggested here are primarily aimed at sewing machine stitching, but hand stitching can, with care, be used effectively or to add extra surface embellishments after machine stitching.

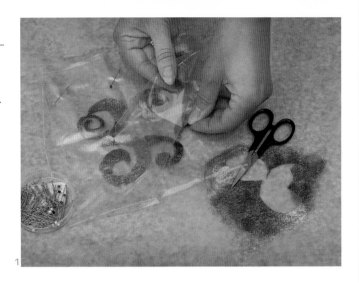

1 Cut shapes out of sheets of pre-bonded Angelina and pin these onto a sheet of cold water soluble. Place this into an embroidery frame.

Stitch around the edges of the Angelina shapes and between them so that you create a lacy structure with areas of Angelina.

Place the fabric into a bowl of warm water and leave for the soluble fabric to dissolve away. The time involved depends upon the weight of your chosen soluble fabric - from a few minutes to half an hour. Change the water at least once during the process. Remove and allow to dry. If the piece still feels sticky as it dries, then some soluble fabric remains on your work and you might need to re-soak the piece.

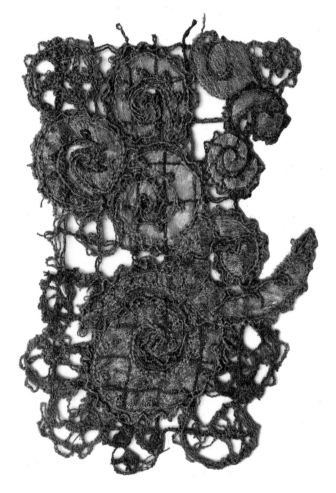

2 Take cut sections of Angelina fabrics, randomly chopped and sprinkled on their own or add other snips of fabrics, threads, sequins, etc., to make a sandwich between two layers of cold water soluble.

Pin or tack the sandwich together to stop the pieces moving too much whilst stitching. Place into an embroidery frame.

Stitch into the sandwich either by hand or by machine, randomly or in a specific pattern until the pieces are all securely trapped. Then dissolve the fabric and dry the piece as described above.

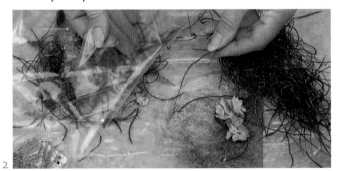

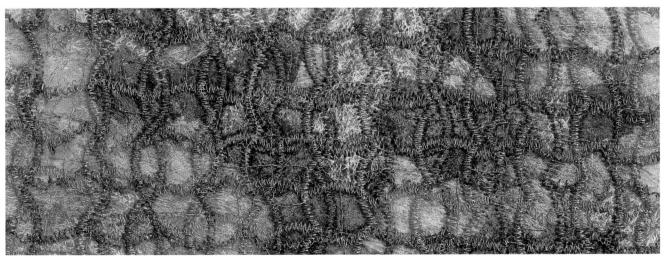

3 Here we are able to exploit to the full the properties of both soluble fabrics and the fusing and colour changing of the 'Hot Fix' Angelina fibres. The idea is flexible enough to accommodate both hand and machine stitchers.

To create an 'angelically' sheer fabric from the Angelina fibres, lay un-bonded 'Hot Fix' Angelina fibres into a sandwich of soluble fabric, pin or tack to hold and place the sandwich into an embroidery frame.

Then stitch by hand or machine or both to hold the fibres and to create patterns across the surface.

Dissolve the water soluble fabric away and allow the fibres and stitching to dry.

When dry, iron the piece between baking parchment to fuse the fibres as normal.

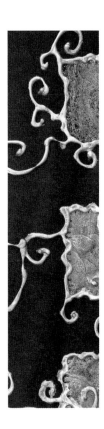
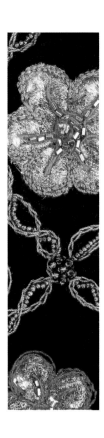
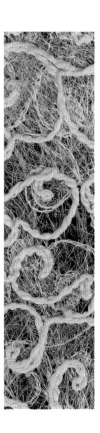

- voluptuous vessels
- sumptuous slip
- shimmering appliqué
- angelic wrap

testing the water

Included here is a selection of projects chosen to utilise a wide range of the unique properties of Angelina fibres. All with titles designed to make you groan!

The first, **Voluptuous Vessels**, uses the trapping properties of the 'Hot Fix' fibres as described in **Centre of Attraction** and involves no stitching. It should take you no more than an hour as described, though of course there are many additional embellishments you could make to personalise this or any of the other projects.

The second, **Sumptuous Slip**, again involves a minimum of stitch, but introduces appliqué and gilding into the equation.

The third project, **Shimmering Appliqué** jumps up a rung in complexity, but is composed from simple applied elements that look stunning and appear much more complex than they really are.

The final project, the **Angelic Wrap**, does require you to be familiar with your sewing machine and, in this form, to be able to do cable stitch on your machine. But it's well worth the effort – see for yourself.

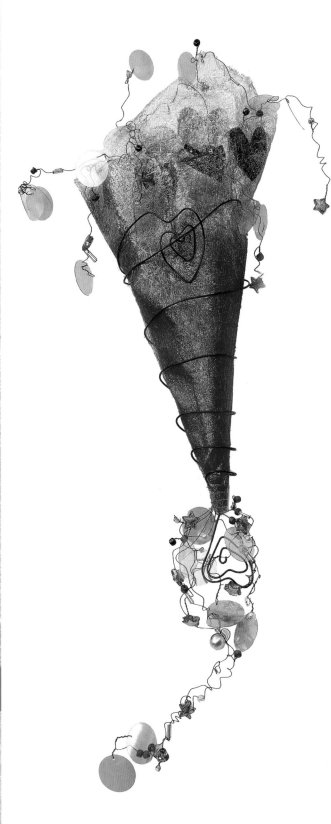

A completely mad and 'over the top' project for starters using the properties of trapping and shaping which are possible with the 'Hot Fix' fibres. The Angelina gives a radiant surface, the wires give strength, form and decoration, and the beads and sequins finish off the fun.

Either of these vessels makes fun accessories for table centres on special occasions, perhaps filled with sweets or little favours, or to hang on trees at Christmas. They could be made on a smaller scale as wonderful 'wedding favours' or to distribute to guests at other festivities.

Once you have tried the instructions given here, think about adding other materials into the 'sandwich', or more wires for decoration, or adding stitch. What about burning into the Angelina with a hot wire to make lacy edges, or beading around the vessels? Don't stop at the basics, make these your own special vessels.

Equipment you will need:
For both vessels:
Iron
Ironing pad
Baking parchment
Sewing pins
Kebab stick or similar

Materials you will need:
3 colours of 'Hot Fix' Angelina approx. 3g (½ small bag) each of Ultra Violet, Key Lime and Raspberry (or choose your own mixture)
Thin wire such as beading wire or craft wire in 24 gauge or 0.3mm diameter. At least 6 lengths between 16 and 24" (40 – 60cm) long. The more wires you add, the more decoration you can add at the last stage
A selection of beads and sequins to match your colour scheme

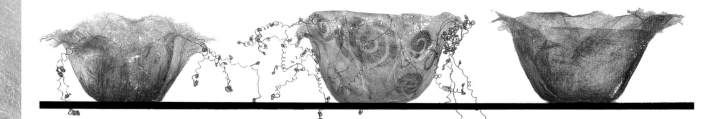

doing it... a bowl shaped voluptuous vessel

In addition, for the bowl, you will need:
A bowl shaped 'former' with fairly steep sides such as a plastic steamed pudding container. This should be covered in baking parchment.

1 Make a small piece of Angelina fabric from the Ultra Violet fibres 4 – 6" (10 – 15cm) square. Cut small motifs or patterns out of this piece of fabric, these might be squares, hearts, spirals, triangles, etc. Put these on one side for a moment.

2 Lay out approximately half of the other 2 colours of Angelina into a circle or a square. By the time you are done the exact shape will not be noticeable. You could use one of the colours around the edges as shown. Lay your patterns cut from the original fabric around your piece, either in a pattern or randomly. The wires now need laying across your Angelina so that they cross in the centre. Pin the wires down some distance away from the fibres or you will find that they bounce around. Spread the remaining fibres over the top of your piece. Place baking parchment over the work and iron (iron set to silk setting) but only just touch the iron onto the paper, so that the fibres are just fused on the outer layer and are not yet fully forming a fabric. Remove pins and very carefully take the fabric off the ironing pad.

Here's a tip .....
Because you are only very lightly ironing the fibres, they may need to be very carefully turned over whilst still inside the baking parchment and ironed gently on the reverse side to make it handleable.

3 Lay the Angelina piece over the bowl shape (which should be covered in baking parchment) and tuck the protruding wires under the bowl.

4/5 Now fold a piece of baking parchment over the Angelina, also tucking the ends of the baking parchment under the bowl. Iron until fixed. This may need a fair amount of pressure and you may need to repeatedly take off the outer parchment to check that all the fibres have fused.

6 Once all of the fibres have been fused, slide beads and sequins onto the free ends of the thin wires, twisting each bead into place along the wires. Then for added twist, wrap each thin wire around the kebab stick, slide the stick out and manipulate the wire into a position to suit you.

1/2

3

Materials you will need:

See materials list for the bowl project on page 26. For the Cornucopia, you will also need: A 6" (15cm) square of card or stiff plastic rolled to a point in one corner to form a cone and then taped into shape.

1 Make a piece of Angelina fabric from the Ultra Violet fibres around 4 – 6"(10 – 15cm) square. Cut small motifs or patterns out of this piece of fabric and put on one side for a moment.

2 Lay out approximately half of the other 2 colours of Angelina in a simple pattern to form a square shape about 6"(15cm) across. Lay your patterns cut from the Ultra Violet fabric along two adjoining edges. These will become the top lip of your cornucopia.

Place your lengths of wire across the fibres in a bundle, starting below the bottom apex of the square (that is, the corner furthest away from the two edges you have just decorated with the Ultra Violet shapes). From this bottom corner, open up the bundle of wires and spread them fan-like across the fibres allowing the wires to protrude from the top and bottom of the square. As with the bowl project, the wires now need pinning into place away from the fibres. Spread another layer of fibres over the top of this one, reserving just a little fibre for a finishing procedure. Place baking parchment over the work and iron (iron set to silk setting) to fuse the fibres into a fabric. Remove pins and take the fabric off the ironing pad.

3 Wrap the square around the 'former' made from a cone of plastic or card, placing the remaining Angelina fibre into the overlap.

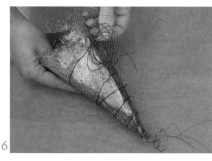

5

4/5 Place a piece of baking parchment over the top and iron over the overlap until fixed (as quickly and lightly as possible to avoid over-heating the fibres). This stage feels at first as though you might need an extra hand, but it is possible if you hold the work as shown.

6 The cornucopia will need a little extra support, so take the thick wire to wrap around from the base of the cornucopia to about ¾ of the height of the cornucopia. Leave a little at the bottom and twist the wire at the top around the previous wrap of wire and form a little hook or loop. You may find that this stage takes a little 'jiggling' to get just right.

Here's a tip....
You may find this easier with a pair of small pliers.

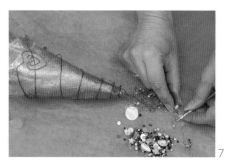

6

7 Take the cornucopia off the former and slide beads and sequins onto the free ends of the thin wires, twisting each bead into place along the wires. Using the kebab stick, twist and manipulate the free wires as for the bowl.

7

sumptuous slip

A lovely combination of rich blue velvet embellished with a richly textured surface to create a book cover. This is another easy project with a bare minimum of stitching.

You can of course use other colour combinations. Another successful colour mix is to use Forest Blaze 'Hot Fix' Angelina with a dark green velvet and copper or gold relief outliner. The combinations of simple geometric shapes outlined with curling scrolls of the outliner are many and varied. If you then think about adding the wide variety of colours available in Angelina, velvets, outliners and transfer foils you can create pretty much endless combinations! What about additional stitching or beading onto the cover?

Equipment you will need:
Iron
Baking parchment
Ironing pad
Needle, standard sewing thread, small scissors

Materials you will need:
Blue velvet; twice as long as the distance around the outside of your book and 1½"(4cm) wider
Wisteria 'Hot Fix' Angelina (Half of a 7g pack)
Small sections of textured threads or fabrics in golds (I have used scraps of scrunched silk/metal tissue)
Iridescent pale blue relief outliner
3" (10cm) square piece of gold transfer foil
A book to cover

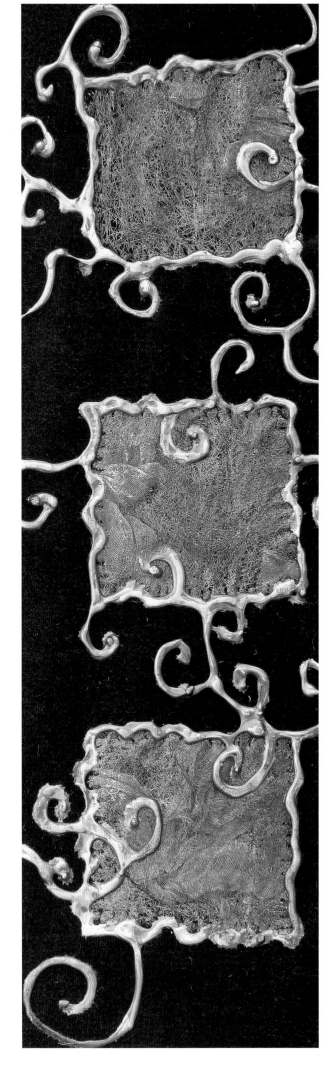

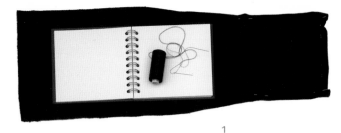

1

2

3

4

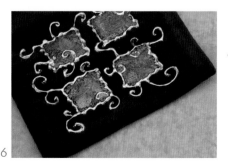

5

6

1 Hem around the velvet allowing approximately ½"(1.25 cm) top and bottom, above and below the book's overall size so that it is not too tight to slip over when finished. Fold the ends in until they wrap around the book comfortably and leave sufficient gap in the centre for both the spine and for the cover to be pulled on or off. This will be approximately ¾ of the length of the cover from outer edge towards the spine. With the cover inside out, slip stitch the outer edges top and bottom from the reverse side then turn through.

2 Lay a first layer of Wisteria 'Hot Fix' Angelina onto baking parchment and sprinkle with the textured threads or fabric scraps. Lay another layer of Angelina over the top and iron to fix as usual.

Here's a tip ...
You will probably need to iron the Angelina fibres lightly on both sides to trap in the fabric or other scraps.

3 Cut from this 4 small squares (their size will depend upon the size of the book and whether you want to lay the pieces in a square or another simple geometric design) onto the front of the cover. These can then be pinned and stitched into place with simple slip stitching.

Here's a tip ...
Beware – the Angelina fabric, like so many other fabrics likes to move as it is stitched onto the velvet. So pin or tack well before stitching the squares into place.

4 Open the bottle of outliner with as small a hole in the tip as possible to achieve a thin line of glue. Decorate around the edge of the Angelina squares and onto the velvet with lines and swirls of outliner. Allow the glue to dry. This will take a while and it must be completely dry before gilding.

5 Take the sheet of gold transfer foil and place it over the outliner, with a sheet of baking parchment over the top. Iron over this to transfer the gold onto the outliner. Be careful not to press too hard or you might overheat the Angelina and change its colour or adhere transfer foil to the Angelina and neither of these are what we are looking for in this project.

6 Remember to leave the ironed transfer foil to cool for a few seconds after ironing before pulling it away from the surface, as it will come away much more easily once it is cooler and you may need to repeat the ironing of the transfer foil over the outliner a few times until you are happy with the results.

Simply slip the book cover onto your book and your book project is complete.

shimmering appliqué

The intermingling of intricate designs and the patching of finely stitched sections of cloth divided by bold lines all combine to create a characteristically rich Indian-inspired hanging.

This project invites you to try a variety of appliqué techniques using both hand and machine stitching (though it could be adapted for use by hand or machine stitching alone) with discreet beading to further enrich the surface texture.

The collage is built using three different appliqué techniques but surprisingly only one colour of Angelina! It exploits the translucency of the Angelina and that chameleon effect in which different colours of background fabric highlight differences in the Angelina fabric colour

This project also encourages you to exploit the colour changes that happen at different heat applications. As with all of the projects, you may well take on board the principles but work with your own colour schemes, designs and stitch techniques.

Equipment you will need:
Iron
Parchment
Ironing pad
Sewing machine and requisites
Hand sewing requisites
Small Indian print block (Try a few designs before deciding which block to use – blocks which have a good flat surface and clear gaps between seem to work best)

Materials you will need:
Raspberry 'Hot Fix' Angelina 14g (two small bags)
3 background fabrics:
Purple silk satin (10 x 4") (25 x 10cm)
Purple velvet colour 1 (10 x 10") (25 x 25cm)
Purple velvet colour 2 (14 x 6") (35 x 15cm)
Light weight sew-in Vilene approximately 35 x 20" (1 x 0.5m)
Toning purple or orange lightweight fabric approximately 35 x 4" (1m x 10cm) to use as the twisted couched strips between the areas of the collage.
Threads: 2 colours of machine thread to tone with colours of background (I have used gently variegated threads)
2 – 3 thicker hand stitch threads
Beads to tone with the Angelina fibres – mixture of sizes and variations of colour
Chopped pieces of irise paper to trap into one section. (This is sold as 'twinkle snow' at Christmas, or can be chopped from a full sheet, or of course you can find other lightweight materials/papers/sequins to do the same)

The piece is made from three sections joined together at the end, each section is described separately as Pattern 1 (Triangle Appliqué), Pattern 2 (Rosette Appliqué) and Pattern 3 (Flower Appliqué). Then the instructions will lead you through the process of putting the appliqué collage together. If you feel that the machine stitching is pulling or that the fabrics are slipping, then place the pieces in an embroidery frame, though I haven't found this to be necessary.

triangle appliqué

1 Make a small sheet of standard thickness Raspberry 'Hot Fix' Angelina 14 x 6" (35 x 15cm) (Sheet 1), and then a second smaller sheet of the same colour 4 x 6" (10 x 15cm) (Sheet 2). Make a third sheet of standard thickness Raspberry 'Hot Fix' Angelina approximately 4 x 6" (10 x 15cm) but overheat to an orange colour, stopping before the iridescence is gone (Sheet 3).

Lie Sheet 1 of Angelina flat across the purple satin silk background fabric with a layer of lightweight sew-in Vilene behind.

Cut 10 elongated triangles from Sheet 3 and the same number of smaller triangles from Sheet 2, then pin these across the background with the smaller triangles placed on top of the larger ones.

2 Now stitch around the triangles with a single straight sewing line. Edge all of these with a small (approximately 1.5 stitch width) zigzag satin stitch using threads in orange and purple tones.

3 Using the hand threads in orange, stitch between the triangles using herringbone stitch.

rosette appliqué

1 Lay lightweight sew-in Vilene behind the piece of purple velvet 14 x 6"(35 x 15cm). Press Raspberry 'Hot Fix' Angelina onto the print block you have chosen (as described in **Making a Good Impression** on page 11/12) and make several until you have 10 that you are happy with. Remember to make full use of your fibres and as you make one of the prints, trim away the edges and use these trimmings as some of the Angelina for the next print.

Pin the impressed Angelina shapes in a staggered line onto the velvet taking up no more than 3" (8cm) of the width of the background fabric. Stitch the impressed shapes onto the purple velvet with a wavy machine line. Follow the outline of your shape a few times to blend in the edge of the impressed rosettes with the background fabric.

2 Taking a blending colour of a thicker thread, hand stitch in seeding stitches all over the velvet.

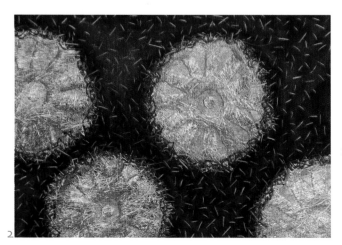

flower appliqué

1 Make a sheet of raspberry 'Hot Fix' Angelina with chopped irise film, or similar, trapped into it by laying down a light layer of the Angelina onto baking parchment covering an area approximately 8" (20cm) square, then sprinkle on the chopped irise film and lay over another thin layer of fibres. Cover and iron as usual.

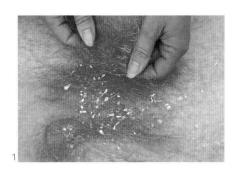

2 Take a 10" (25cm) square piece of sew-in Vilene. Draw a grid onto the Vilene approximately 3" (7cm) wide in square shapes, then draw a circle at each of the joins and small ovals along the lengths of the sides. In the centre of each of the squares draw a simple flower shape with a circular centre and six petals as shown.

Take the 10" (25cm) square piece of dark purple velvet, place the Vilene which has the design drawn onto it behind the fabric and pin into place. Stitch with a standard toning thread from the reverse over the wavy lines making the grid (ignore the flower shapes for now). This can be achieved either by hand in a small running stitch or using free stitching on the sewing machine. You can then follow the pattern in a hand stitching thread using chain-stitch.

3 Cut 12 2" (4cm) squares of the Angelina fabric you have just made and place this in the centre of each grid square over the space where you have drawn the flower on the reverse. Hold each in place with a couple of pins away from the flower outlines. Stitch from the reverse using a toning thread in around the flower shapes, this is probably most secure if machined. Turn over and trim around the shapes.

4 Free machine stitch, cable stitch or hand couch around the flower shapes on the right side of the fabric and add details in similar stitching with a contrasting thread. Add beads to the flowers and the grid lines as you wish to create a lovely sumptuous surface for this section, which will be the focus of your finished piece.

Putting the piece together

Lay the three pieces onto another piece of sew-in Vilene, in the positions as seen in the picture of the finished piece to make a square. Make sure that the edges butt up together and then catch them down either by hand or by machine.

Take the piece of 4" (10cm) wide thin fabric and twist it into a cord. Then couch it down with bold stitches along the joins of the sections.

To finish

Your piece could be placed in a frame with a mount, or make a soft hanging by backing the piece with lining fabric, adding a sleeve for a hanging rod and edging with a French hem of a toning fabric.

The design lends itself to be extended by making more sections and piecing them together. Other uses might include the centre of a cushion, a bag, a purse, a dress decoration for a special occasion etc!

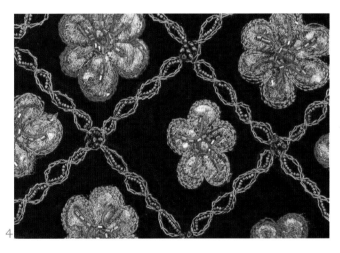

A deliciously refined stole or wrap, which would be eminently suitable for wearing on special occasions. I made a special one that matched an outfit I wore to a friend's Silver Wedding celebration and it was much commented on, so you can expect your results to be admired too.

You will be using more advanced machine embroidery combining sheer fabrics and one of the cold water soluble techniques described in **Dissolving Passions**. Taking the theme further, you could also make bags and other accessories to match.

Equipment you will need:
Sewing machine and requisites, including a standard sewing foot and a darning foot if you have one
Scissors
Sewing pins
Baking parchment
Iron
Ironing pad
Flat embroidery frame and silk pins

Materials you will need:
75 x 24" (2m x 60cm) silk mousseline
14g (2 x 7g bags) Crystal Blaze 'Hot Fix' Angelina fibres
Natural coloured machine embroidery thread
A thicker natural coloured thread for cable stitching
Lightweight cold water soluble fabric; 2 pieces 14 x 12"(35 x 30cm) and 2 pieces 14 x 22"(35 x 45cm)

Useful equipment and materials

doing it

1 Take the silk mousseline, fold it in half lengthways and seam down the long side. Then turn to right side, iron flat and seam over the top to make a French seam. Cut the two ends to whatever angle you find agreeable. Take one of the smaller pieces of cold water soluble and lay the Angelina fibres across it relatively thinly. Place one end of the wrap onto the Angelina fibres.

2 Lay another fine layer of 'Hot Fix' Angelina fibres over the top of the fabric by about 4" (10cm).

3 Fold the other smaller piece of the cold water soluble over the top of this to create a sandwich. Pin or tack this sandwich into place. Secure a section of the wrap end onto your frame.

Using free machine embroidery with a normal embroidery thread and the darning foot in place, stitch swirls (or other shapes) moving the frame as necessary and stitching randomly up into the scarf to blend the join of the mousseline fabric and the Angelina.

Make up the other end of the wrap in the same way.

4 The raised stitching has been achieved here using cable stitching. To work like this you will need to loosen the tension screw on your bobbin case by approximately ½ a turn and fill several bobbins with the thicker thread you have chosen.

Test the stitching on a spare piece of fabric. You are aiming to get a smooth line of thicker thread along the underside of the line, looking like a hand stitched line. If the bobbin tension is too tight it will drag and tend to jam in the machine, if too loose it will make a knobbly loose line and also tend to jam!

5 When you are happy with the stitch, stitch similar patterns to echo the original stitching onto the wrap and the soluble film ends using the cable stitching. As with the standard thread, ensure that your stitching works randomly up into the body of the wrap to integrate the two surfaces.

The soluble fabric helps to stop the delicate silk puckering so make sure that you cover the fabric or add other patches as you go. At this stage, the two sets of stitching should be holding the Angelina fibres temporarily in place.

6 Snip away any loose ends. Place the entire wrap into warm water, laying it as flat as possible and leave for at least 20 minutes, changing the water after the first 5 minutes. Remove from the water and allow to dry.

7 Place the scarf between layers of baking parchment and iron on silk setting to fuse the Angelina fibres and to neaten the silk mousseline.

Lastly, trim or melt with a hot wire around the protruding sections of Angelina fabric and 'it's a wrap'!

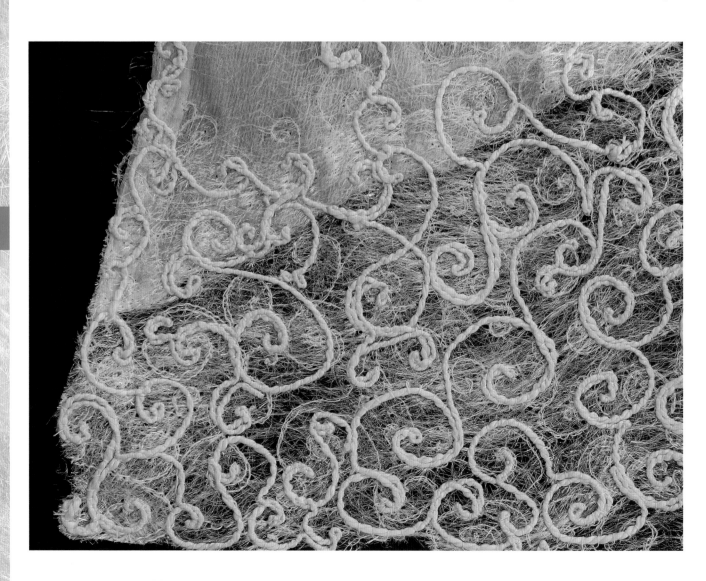

- dawn armitage-hoyer
- mavis howard
- liz welch
- alysn midgelow-marsden

hot dates!

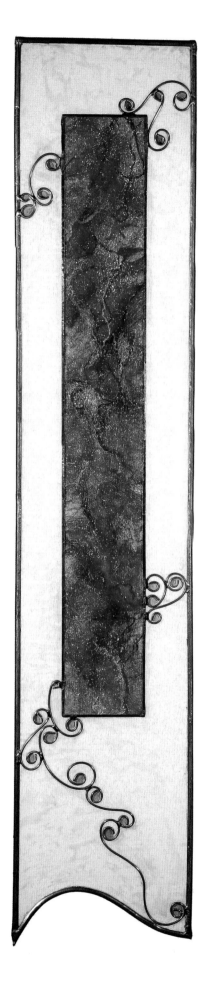

Dawn says:
'I make glass and silk panels for walls, windows and tables.

I am inspired by the colours and patterns within water ripples, reflections and rainbows and interpret this in my self-developed lamination technique, which involves setting silk fibres into glass giving a feel of contemporary stained glass. The pieces are then embellished with gilding, etching and metal wires.

I am continually exploring other materials to combine with the silks, one of these being Angelina fibres. Through experimentation I have found that Angelina gives a uniquely lustrous sheen and an iridescence, which gives my work the lovely watery feel I wanted. The fibres blend beautifully with the silk fibres to complement and enhance my pieces.'

mavis howard

Mavis says:

'Having learnt my sewing skills at my mother's knee (I made my own and my daughters' wedding dresses), I was introduced to creative machine embroidery at a day workshop. What a revelation!

I am now producing pieces that have been influenced by functionality – cuffs, collars, shoes, etc. – but with a theatrical feel. My inspiration comes from the colours of India.

For me, Angelina works best when used sparingly and overlaid with chiffon or held concealed by stitching. It was particularly suitable for the slipper and the collars, where I wanted an opulent effect, but subtle glints rather than glitter.

I love using Angelina - it is so versatile and exciting – but most of all, it is fun!'

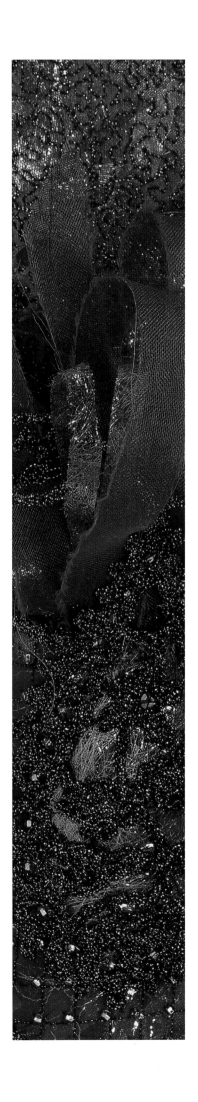

Liz says of her work:
'As a textile artist and maker of jewellery, I love to explore and experiment with new materials that excite me.

For 12 years I have been developing and expressing my ideas using fabric and mixed media, in particular Friendly Plastic.

Having discovered Angelina, it seemed a natural companion to my work, adding texture, sparkle and interest in subtle ways and sometimes in bold and delightfully brash ways.

Generally I use the Angelina as a very fine open mesh for extruding the Friendly Plastic through to give texture, but occasionally in thicker form to add accents of sparkle.'

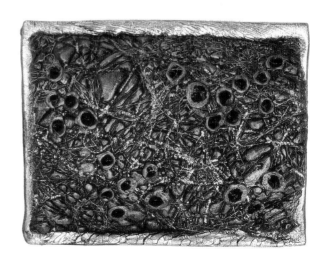

alysn midgelow marsden

Just in case you haven't heard enough about my dalliance with Angelina, here's another story. This commissioned piece has caused a few smiles.

Made as a wedding anniversary present from a wife to her husband, the centres are sugar cubes the lady had saved from their honeymoon seven years earlier. Surely, she said to me, we can do better than see them sitting in a jar forever!

Well, some head scratching followed about the best way to preserve a sugar cube for posterity. Do you mean that this has never crossed your mind before?

We devised this simple but effective piece.

Each sugar cube has been preserved and gilded, then gently cupped into the centre of slightly melted Angelina and wire baskets. The baskets are applied onto a dark velvet background and the words 'they were but sweet, but figures of delight' (a quote from a Shakespearean sonnet) sinuously curves around them.

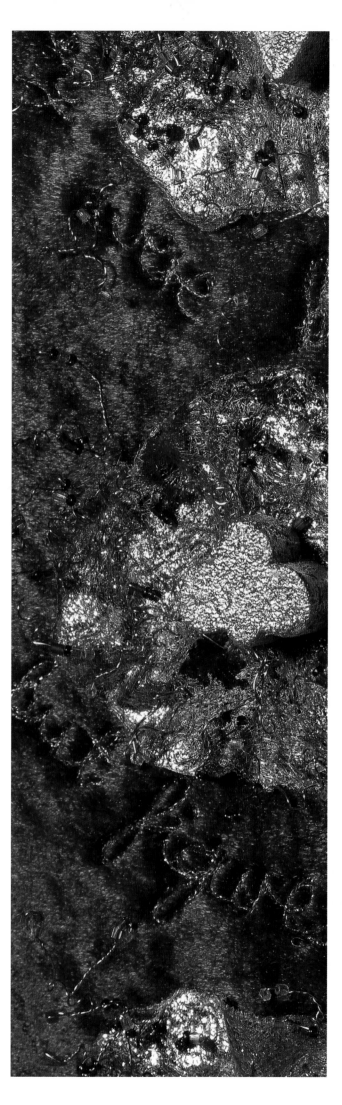